Alphabet Movers

written by
Teresa Benzwie

illustrated by
Robert Bender

National Dance Education Organization

Text Copyright © 2002 by Teresa Benzwie
Illustrations Copyright © 2002 by Robert Bender

Published in the United States by:
National Dance Education Organization
4948 St. Elmo Avenue #301
Bethesda, MD 20814-6013
301-657-2880

Library of Congress Cataloging-in-Publication Number 2001094458
Benzwie, Teresa
Alphabet Movers by Teresa Benzwie
Illustrated by Robert Bender

Summary: Children learn the shapes and
sounds of the alphabet while having fun
and developing their bodies, minds,
and self-esteem.

ISBN: 1-930798-08-3

Typesetting by Matt Varrato
First Edition 2001

Printed in the USA
on acid-free paper

The full-color art was produced with animator's paint on two layers of acetate,
which was applied with stencil brushes.

For Harlene Galen, Ed.D.
inspired educator, generous and devoted friend

Special Thanks:
    to Robert Bender for his magical illustrations
    to Stephanie Lees for dancing through these pages
    to Jane Bonbright, Ed.D. and Rima Faber, Ph.D. at NDEO
        for supporting and believing in this work
    to Rabbi Marcia Prager for her many blessings and skilled editing help

A is **all** about **action**

The **a**lphabet begins with letter **A**
You may move in every way

B is for bounce

Can you **b**ounce up and down like a **b**all?
Bounce yourself large
Bounce yourself small

C is for **c**rawl **c**limb and **c**uddle

Crawl like a **c**aterpillar
Climb like a **c**at
Cuddle up **c**lose
You **c**an do that

D is for **d**ancer

Dream you are **d**ancing **d**ancing
Turning round and round
Are you **d**izzy?
Dance up and **d**own

E is for **e**njoying **e**xercise

How **e**xciting you can be
when you use your **e**nergy

F is for falling floating flopping

What fun!
Can you **fall float flop** without a stop?

G is for **grow**

Go go go!
Take steps so **grand**
Stretch and **grow** like a rubber band

H is for **h**op

Hippity **h**op **h**igh
Hoppity **h**ip low
Show you are **h**appy
Ho **h**o **h**o!

I is for **i**magine

I can **i**magine
      being an **i**nchworm **i**nching so slow
        being **i**vy climbing high and low

J is for **jump**

Jump forward   **j**ump back
Jump up and down like a **j**umping **j**ack

K is for **k**ick

Kick **k**ick **k**ick high in the air
Kicking here **k**icking there
Kicking **k**icking everywhere

L is for leap

Large leaps   little leaps
Leap high   leap low
Leap fast   leap slow

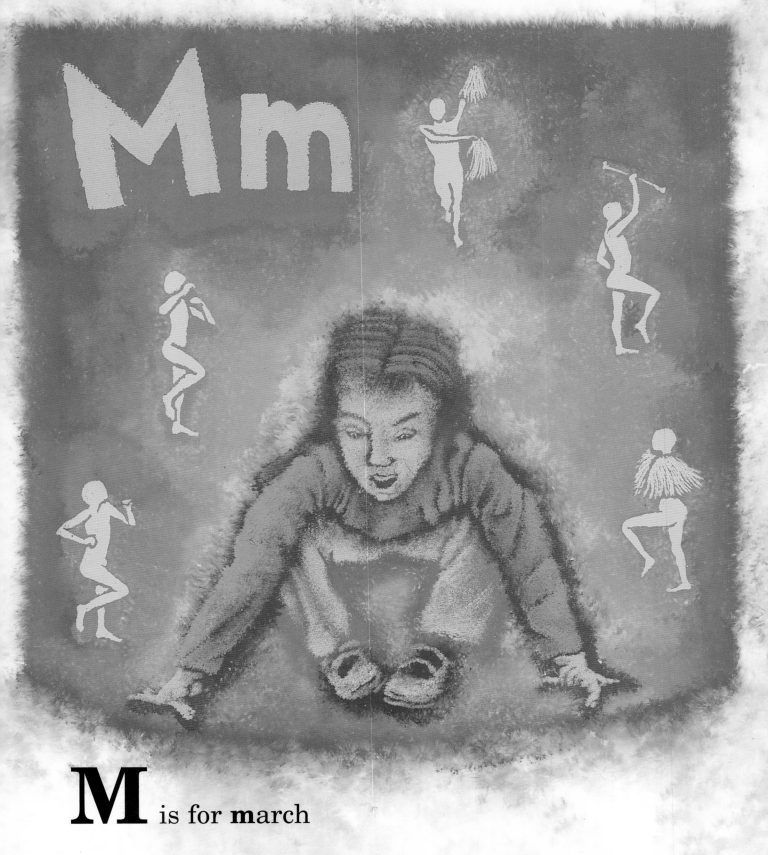

M is for **m**arch

March to the **m**usic
Lift each knee
March to the beat so **m**errily

N is for **ni**mble

Now be **ni**mble
Bend your k**n**ees
Dance your **n**ame as you please

O is for **on off o**ut and **o**ver

Jump **on off** and **o**ut **o**f the **O**
Oops!
Over you go

P is for **p**ush **p**ull and **p**ounce

Point and **p**ress
Peek and **p**lay
Do it all your own way

Q is for **q**uick

Can you be so **q**uick and **q**uiet?
Let's see you try it

R is for **r**olling **r**eaching and **r**unning a **r**ace

Are you **r**eady?
Get into place

S is for simply silly

Can you **s**mile **s**queeze **s**weep **s**tamp?
Can your body **s**tretch and **s**wing?
You can do most anything

T is for turn

Turning turning tip toe touch
Can you twist?
How much?

U is for **u**p and **u**nder

Up through a hoop **u**nder a table
Move around as much as you're able

V is for **vibrate**

Vibrate and shake
Vibrate with every step you take

W is for **wiggle wriggle walk** and **wind**

What other movements can you find?

X is for **X** marks the spot

Use part of your body to draw an **X** in the air
Going from there to here
and here to there

Y is for **y**ell

Make a **Y** with **y**our body
Yell **y**ippity **y**i **y**ea!
Yes **y**es **y**ou did it.
Good work for today!

Z is for **z**oom

Zooming through space
Zig **z**ag **z**ig **z**ag
Back into place

Children naturally learn through movement. *Alphabet Movers* encourages total involvement of body and mind in the learning process.

Try these experiences to make the book come alive and grow.

More Letter Experiences

• Shape a letter, first using your hands, fingers or arms and then forming the shape with your body as in the book. You can do this lying down, sitting or standing. Try it with a partner or with a larger group.

• Dance from A to Z shaping your body from one letter to the next, while moving through the room. Use the letters in your name, creating a name dance. Add some lively music.

• Dance in a group. Each dancer shapes one letter so that together you will spell a word or name. One of you can be a sculptor and form the others into shapes of the letters. You may also recombine yourselves to form new words.

• Imagine that different parts of the body, such as an elbow, nose or foot, are a crayon or paintbrush with which to draw in the air. Draw the letters in space using different rhythms.

• Find movement-rich words or images beginning with each of the letters. For example, act out two or three silly words together such as flying frogs, floating fish or fancy feathers. Use parts of the body such as funny faces, fidgety fingers, flopping feet or falling freckles.

• Make a dance using a series of words beginning with a specific letter. The S dance can be stretching, skipping and slinking used over and over again. Add music or rhythm instruments to go with these word dances.

• Draw letters on the playground with chalk. If you are indoors, shape the letter on the floor with yarn or masking tape. Walk, skip, hop, crawl or jump following the shapes and saying the sounds.

• Lie down on large paper, shaping the first letter of your name. A friend can trace your outline and then you can fill it in by drawing your face and clothes. Paste on pictures of things beginning with your letter.

• Place letters on the floor. Jump, hop, leap or skip from letter to letter spelling out some word.

• While in the shape of a letter, see how many ways you can move and dance. Try this alone or with a partner.

Have fun, create and dance your own letter ideas!